Putting Life on Paper

HPJ's Writeeasy Publishing

ISBN (Trade pbk.) 978-1-7330502-0-3

Layout and Design: Chris Massenburg

Cover Art: Aimee Bridges

BCST logo: Asia Sampson

HPJ's Writeeasy Publishing

Durham, North Carolina

www.dasanahanu.com   www.bullcitypoetryslam.com

The Bull City Slam Team (BCST) is the Triangle's regional and national competing poetry slam team. The members of the team are selected at the Jambalaya Soul Slam, a monthly poetry slam series that is a part of poetry programming at the Hayti Heritage Center in Durham, NC. The BCST is honored to be supported by the St. Joseph's Historic Foundation.

Poets featured in this chapbook include:

Wendy Jones, Dasan Ahanu, Brandon "Ishine" Evans, Eric "LB" Thompson, Lejuane "El'Ja" Bowens, and Micah Romans

Table of Contents

Calypso's Tale
Ishine

The way the ocean breathed hello and goodbye
In its waves to the beach.
Where we sat sun-burnt for hours,
skin seasoned and wrinkled
from the lust we floated in
we were never meant to last.
Only built to preserve the beautiful painting
that had long been auctioned off to the highest bidder.
Sometimes,
the hardest part of a relationship
is knowing when to throw the anchor.
When to realize the tide is never coming in
and rock bottom is speaking loudly at your feet.
Your ship set sail without me,
but if you find her,
the girl with salt in her hair;
Calypso,
with a tsunami in her chest
beating against the willpower of men
like piers
like hearts
they all eventually break;
shatter into pieces of memories
that we to put back together and call art.
We try to find beauty in the broken things
Tell her she taught me so much.
Taught me that forever sounds so much longer
on the breath of a child.
That some lessons grow up with us,
like in grade school:
I learned that hearts are symmetrical
could you find the twin I gave away?
This half of a heart looks more like a question that
nobody seems to know the answer to.
I've read that identical twins have the same DNA,

but different fingerprints.
Calypso,
our hearts never fit right together.
We left a different imprint on each others lives.
You bellowing volcano,
every woman I used to forget you
always asked why there is so much blackness on my
heart
An eruption waiting on your tongue
The fallout was always worse then the argument
I'm still cleaning all the ash you spewed into my life
Is our artwork beautiful to you yet?
If the walls in your old apartment could speak,
I bet there would be holes in their speech from where my
fists hit,
from where my words gave up.
I could never save you from yourself..
the story of a martyr doesn't sound so beautiful from the
lips of the one dying.
Saving people always comes at the price of a life,
and I wasn't willing to die for you.
I knew our union was dead when the heartbeat of our
love
Sounded like the day we when shopping for shorts long
enough
to cover the flat lines you carved into your thighs.
When you told me you would do it again.
When I caught you praying to your toilet,
you said you were just correcting God's design.
I was too afraid of giving up on you.
A dandelion flailing in the wind
The heart of a serial killer
questioning why its working so hard to keep this monster
going
No one wants to say its over.
I am sorry I am just like the men in my family
my grandfather telling his wife that my mother is just
imagining things

the boogeyman doesn't smell like his cologne
her goosebumps are just a reaction
and not her body warning her to be afraid
before she knows what to fear
my mother wondering
if the skeletons in my dads closet would come out before
he did
me telling you ill always be there for you
I guess Adams apple is still causing men
to make the wrong decisions.
You were eve
I was an orange hanging from the tree of the knowledge
you never picked me first
when sex is the only thing holding your relationship
together
you begin to question what the condom is really
protecting you from
no matter how much you peeled back my layers
you could never find a seed in my core.
You natural disaster
A tsunami in your chest
A volcano waiting on your breath
Your lava filled words just keep building the island you've
created for yourself
Stop trying to find love in every sailor arms
In every man that washed up on your shores
Castaways aren't meant to stay
Love the sand in your eyes
They are as many as the reasons you can find beauty in
your deserted reflection
Calypso,
has your fish net flesh caught enough men yet
My seashell of a heart just wants you to hear what's
inside
Calypso
You were just a chapter in my story
Your words
Will always be on the pages of my spine

Love will have you believing that an island is the whole world
But there is so much more
So much more

Remnant Patch
Wendy Jones

Because the spirit will recognize the truth
by the spirit
and I was told to remind you
Once upon...
when it happened
when the sun went dark
when the clouds rumbled
with the sounds of feathers and metal clashing
of screaming
he saw it
was standing on a mountain side
contemplating the relation of time
to the expanse of the sky
considering the works of a man's life that would deem
him worthy of heaven
when it happened
he saw it
giants falling from the sky
wings burning
cursing their creator
and man whom he loved so much
their beautiful faces
permanently twisted
by rage and horror
when it happened
when they were cast from heaven
when the morning star
fell dark
when disenfranchised angels
became demons
bent on destruction
running in every direction
guided by vengeance
he saw it
his eyes burnt from the sight of it

so that he could see nothing
but the birth of evil
he ran home to tell his people
but they had already broken bread
with these that had fell
and sold all they had to sell
in Sodom
In Gomorra he found
that heaven held no appeal
to the instant gratification
of a left hand deal
and so the fallen
bade the people ill
until they too fell
He watched
in horror
opened up his mouth to speak warning
was told he had lied
tried to tell them
to protect their children
to protect their souls
and was told to go
and so he traveled
the expanse of the sky
measured time by its motion
trying to find someone who would listen
who knew more than he
on protecting his people from falling
and when there was no more
new sky for him to see
when his bones had seen
too much time
he fell to his knees and prayed
that God would send someone
to come and keep his people safe
God hears prayers
heard him when
the weary witness

begged for help
So moved was he by this
selfless prayer
That he took his crown from off his head
and in this crown
was 144 thousand gems
illuminated with all the love he had for man
and he shook o
till them gems fell out their settings
and in his hand
and he threw the gems from heaven
to the mercy of the wind
a candle and a match
for the middle of the night
It has been long since the history of heaven
has been forgotten
to the minds of men
Since gems like seeds
fell from heaven
thrown to the mercy of the winds
by the hand of God
in the form of men
they have blended with the blood
they have rooted and blossomed
under the dirt and trash of time
biding there's
for an eternity of moments
waiting to be found
sleeping warriors
We, my brothers and I
woke up one dawn
with our forefathers' memories
remnants of heavens history
dreams
the taste of prayer in dead tongues
we cannot spit enough to get it out
We graceful lunatics
stay with our heads bent

looking on the ground
for something precious and lost
compulsively
we scream at the earth for it move   .
"My brother is buried alive"
"My brother is buried alive"
WE humble scavengers
dig through the earth looking for answers
fear not dirty hands
we put dusty fingers to our lips
and taste purpose
We seekers
look in the eyes for like
for the gleam of gems
pluck them
teach them how to shine
how to seek and scavenge
how to navigate through the history of heaven
teach them to heed the spirit
to pluck gems with care
catch the fallen by their heart
and to help your brother stand
to have care, shine bright
the war is coming
there is a war coming
seek scavenge and shine
learn your lessons well
seek scavenge and shine
learn your lessons well

Baleen Whales
Micah

So, my voice has been cracking since the seventh grade,
I'm used to the surprise on people's faces when such a deep voice,
Rumbles out of this lean frame.
But with all this AUDITORY POWER...

It still surprises me,
When I'm misunderstood.

I feel like I'm on a different wavelength.

But I read an article a while ago that about a certain whale.

Baleen whales can only communicate within the frequencies of 12-25 hertz.
In 2004, though, the NY Times wrote an article about a baleen whale that lived in seclusion, with a voice,
Measured,
At 52 hertz.

At best that's a 27 hertz difference

Now it must be lonely to scream at the top of your lungs,
And still be heard by nobody.

It's the saddest whale song

It was speculated that this whale's voice may have matured over time,
Or that it may have some malformation
Or maybe this whale is deaf
But Dr. Kate Stafford, a researcher at the Marine Mammal Laboratory

Stated that the fact that this individual had survived so
long in such a harsh environment indicates,

That there is nothing wrong with that whale

Now I took this to mean that there is nothing wrong with
the truth.
Its just that sometimes we, as imperfect beings, just can't
hear it.

This is my opinion but maybe,
just maybe, there is nothing wrong with the whale,
Maybe its just every other whale

Because sometimes I sound like a confused typewriter,
and there is no backspace button,
Sometimes you speak and it sounds like a lead guitar,
but with missing strings.
In a sold out concert!
Sometimes the truth speaks and it sounds like…

And that's when I realized that the truth hurts because we
leave it alone too much.

I try to think of a way to communicate with it and I start
stuttering
Draw a blank
And go silent.

But that's when the truth just nods at me.
And smiles.

Because it knows exactly what I mean.
Down to that 52nd hertz

And I realize that being a poet, with a voice that sounds
so different,
Sometimes we all just will not be heard

Like now how many times you come up for air, you will
barely break the surface

And there is so much sky above you.
Land that you will never on.
Patterns of words, stanzas,
Songs that you can sing beautifully!!
 That will never save anyone but yourself

On a stage
Pouring your soul to strangers
Two minutes and 20 seconds into the pain
And all you have left is that 50 second hurt

You can scream, like the day you were born,
Honestly!
Use your lungs like the mere mammal you are
Because you are.

You are the only person who can sing your song as
beautifully as you and
When you're left in that 51st second
You could dic.

And you could die.

And you could die,
But it would be the most truthful and earnest death.

You could die and give truth a reason to keep living
because it didn't feel,
So
…. alone
anymore.

And I don't have to explain my song,
Or my voice to anyone,

As long as it's honest,
Truth can be the only one that hears me.

At the Market
LB

like prisoners traded handcuffs for fences
we bartered away our freedom of speech
i realized this the first time I was called a nigger
anger rooted onto my tongue only to
hang through my teeth
noosed by the knot in my throat
it is so difficult to swallow your heritage sometimes
sometimes words mean so much more than the voice
that carries them
Jesus carried the cross but it was his dying that held the
purpose
and until we can put our hatred to rest
we will continue to burn the cross roads we carry
misdirect the hate in our speech
to have all rights to turn a phrase
to speak louder than out act
but this time I choose to remember
remember
i have the right to remain silent
it cost me everything

Thought Process (A Rictameter)
El'Ja

Maybe
Life has a way
To inform us of when
Luck can become a circumstance
Error can become a gift sent from God
And people see past false pretense
Dressed as extravagance
To mislead you
In faith...

Ugly
Dasan Ahanu

"No object is so beautiful that, under certain conditions, it
will not look ugly."
- Oscar Wilde

I found that to be prophetic
And I offer it to you as you consider
What may seem like a far fetched idea
See I've been thinking that maybe
We've been fooled
I've been looking at the etymology
I'm seeing inconsistencies
I believe that the standards were changed
To reaffirm a false sense of identity
I mean, what if ugly really meant beautiful

Hold on pretty people hear me out
Manufacture used to mean made by hand
Before the barons of industry made it synonymous
With the machinated revolution
Brave used to mean wild, savage, crooked, depraved
The brave new world wasn't a compliment it was a
warning
That all changed when the rape and pillaging of Native
Americans
Became regarded as a heroic accomplishment
So what if ugly really meant beautiful

I looked it up
Why is the word ugly older than pretty, gorgeous
Is it fair
Yes, take a moment and admire the double entendre I
just used
I call it subterfuge
Not what I did, what they are doing to us

The word is older than attractive, appealing, alluring, sexy
It was defined as hateful, dreadful, fearful, and awe
Sounds to me like someone was just pissed and jealous
That somebody refused to conform to narrow-minded perceptions
We are not talking goblins and demons
We are talking about self-determination
Self-assurance, self-confidence
Dammit, why don't we all want to be ugly

What a dastardly trick
They know we are afraid of homonyms, homophones
You know
Bank, crop, sink, slip, UGLY
Words spelled the same, but with different meanings
Pugs...ugly
Nia Long...ugly

I'm saying
Enthusiasm used to mean possessed by God
Now it means possessed by the demons
Of commodity and materialism
You see how the wolves of Wall Street
Tried to put that red riding hood on Obama
And turn Mao into Rumple Stilksken
Taking your first slice of American pie
For spinning working class idealism
Into self determination
I will not be fooled any longer
First King James and now this
They know the error in their ways
Got people using statements like
Diamond in the rough
Like the coal surrounding it ain't black,
But when I bring up fool's gold
Don't nobody want to talk about that

And these damn fairy tales
The ugly duckling that grows into a swan
Hold up Hans Christian Anderson
Who the hell told the swan it was a duckling in the first
place?
Oh, so a long neck, short legs, and broad bill is beautiful
on a swan
But not on Matthew McConaughey
Our fairy godmother has turned the oppression of
patriarchy and heterosexism
Into couture clothing and telephoto lenses

Beauty and the Beast
Just a skinny white woman with someone who looked like
Zach Galifianakis
The Little Mermaid
Just a skinny white woman with bad
decision making skills
Who falls for a dude who can't sail a boat
Where do we learn this stuff?
I'm supposed to trust 2 dudes named Grimm
They are named Grimm but write fairy tales
You can't tell me ugly don't mean beautiful

Sleeping beauty was a narcoleptic
Snow white had snow-white skin, red lips, and dark hair
That's a character on twilight
Propaganda and marketing have been the staple
Of political engagement
McCarthyism
Deception has been the tool of authoritarians
Since the dawn of time
Roswell is real
There were no WMDs
The context changes meaning
Early 70s, Watergate was a political scandal
Today, it'd be an MTV reality show

I now proclaim that everyone should recognize
That you have been duped
You can follow along with the fallacy
But not me
I will no longer conform to the standards of appearance
Set forth by these charlatans
Ugly is beautiful
So if you truly believe
Then say it with me…

U-G-L-Y
I ain't got no alibi
I'm ugly

Stars
Wendy Jones

I imagine our first kiss
A combination of honeysuckles,
razorblades and train wrecks
Full of nervous laughs
The universe will mock us
The stars play hide n seek with the clouds
We made the man in the moon smile
You will hold my hand
Tracing the lifeline in my palm
Trying to find where you fit
One day this will become complicated
There will be silence
Our doubts will remain stuck in our throats
Strangled by fear
There will be declarations of guilt
Questions for God
And a moment of clarity
That reminds us
Time is limited & far too precious to be
wasted on silly things
Like hesitation
Like believing in magic
Like reality
But for now
We will have our first kiss
A fairytale moment that even Disney
couldn't put a visual on
A moment that even a car crash
couldn't metaphor beautiful
A second that will make heaven seem like hell
Our first kiss will be a memory of
New butterflies unquestioning their own wings
Enough to realize flying is better than sitting still
It will be guiltless
It will be trusting someone enough to suck

your heart right out of your chest
And know they will keep it lodged to the roof of their
mouth as long as they live
It will be having faith in you enough not to break me
It will be forever

Braiding My Daughter's Hair
Micah

I raised her to believe that her mind was
a terrible thing to waste.
Sometimes I wonder if it's my fault.
They aimed right at her mind.

And when that didn't work they shot her in her head.

Malala means 'grief stricken'

Israel means 'Triumphant with God'

I want to learn to braid my daughter's hair.
It's on my bucket list.
To be a father that can hold the head of his child with
confidence.
Teach it to maneuver in ways that can't be politic'd away.
I want to be some kids favorite professor.
It's on my bucket list.
To be able to mold their thoughts into realized potential.
Inspire them to eliminate the concept of a box,
and just think outside.
I'm a poet. I want to learn to be the poem.
It's on my bucket list
to take a word and give it life,
meaning.

When a poet has a child, indeed,
that is their masterpiece.
The most beautiful metaphor he could construct.
Comparing the likes of Gandhi to that of Cornell West.
With enough Zora Neale and Rumi in her blood that her
activism comes across as lyrics.

I want her to be the edited version

of the poem God wrote me as.
So she can ghost write a future in which her daughter
can learn without fear of a drive-by lobotomy.

Malala got on her school bus in such a revolutionary way
that it became the Freedom Riders reincarnated.
I want to braid my daughter's hair
for her first day of school.
Walk her to the bus stop and
change the world in the process.

I will tell my students that her kindergarten class will help
me learn to teach them.
That a 16 year old girl w/ lead lined memories can still
envision a tomorrow, despite the grief that may strike.
I will teach them the meaning of "Malala."
And a teenager from Pakistan or a little girl here in
America w/ braided hair can learn to teach others. And
Teach others to learn.

Ziauddin Yousafzai is a poet and a father

I want to name my daughter Israel.
I want it to mean something.
It's on my bucket list.

Love in parts
LB

Part 1 listening for love

She says too often love is likened to the melody
that the radio plays
We inhale the music and exhale its rhythm in our actions
See how we choreograph our speech
We are volume knobs turning ourselves up in hopes to
feel something other than the words

Part 2 listening for life

You grew deaf to my rhythm, heard my music in seeing
his kicks. Wore his soul in the beat of your smile. Named
him before you knew my habit was broken. When a heart
stops beating for a child in belly there is no music only an
instrument that never learned to play.

Space
El'Ja

You can wonder why I carry around this heart-shaped rock with a string around it.
Honestly, you wouldn't understand your own creation
A mad scientist you are
Many moons that are crescents, became full
Something that I should have telescoped when it happened
Magnifying the way your moon was full...of BS
The craters I'm sure came from the errors of men that left imprints in your soul
And like the mass that circles the Earth, you grew cold just like it.
I tried to pull you closer to me
Bring some sort of warmth towards a frigid existence
But science says that we should never interrupt the balance of all things that are placed in its cycle
I decided to pedal right through its plan
Life once inhabited you but now, you're nothing more that a lifeless shell of a former utopia
The dark side is the only side you are willing to show
And I can no longer see where this will lead me
We no longer want to orbit each other in the solar system we created
You used to revolve around me and now your axis is awkward like a hand less thief stealing donuts
Though, this hurts that I've became a drifting star searching for a galaxy to become part of
The only thing I have to stop me for when the right one comes along
Is this heart made of stone tied to an asteroid belt
Hoping that this hardened heart will become the anchor
To a dying world that is continuously floating
Lost in an empty space…

Poem About Myself
Ishine

The first time I rode a bike
My face
Had a personal chat with the concrete
I chipped all my front teeth
Turned my face into a mass murder crime scene
Smiled blood and bone to my mom and said
"I fell"
That night
Nestled between my mother's sobs and Pastor Fred
Price's voice on the television
I drifted to sleep
My mother stayed up the whole night praying over me
When I looked in the mirror the next day
I didn't have a scratch
It's hard not believing in miracles when one stares you in
the face
The first time I saw a vagina.
It was an enlarged computer image thrust before my
eyes by my cousin
The only thing rising faster than my embarrassment
Was my fear at what the fuck was in front of me
We are all afraid
Afraid who we are is okay to be
To be the last one picked for sports or
an empty lunch table
In third grade my lunch table looked like the cast of
Happy Days

The first friend I made was a white boy named Adam
He made Richie Cunningham look like Malcolm X
One time I watched Adam say "Bite me Mom"
I wanted to try it
Got one breath away from unleashing my mom's fury
when my tongue said bite me
It tasted as bittersweet as when I realized
I had spent the whole summer
staying over Adam's house
But not once did he sleep at mine
What was his mother afraid he would learn
Or feel

Would he feel like I did the first time I was asked
"What's your race?"
"What you mixed with"

When your skin
Is as racially ambiguous as mine is
It becomes a melting pot of all of America's mistakes
A multiple choice question
Where every answer is all of the above
A Where's Waldo game
Where everyone is trying to find the white man in your
conundrum of a complexion
You will be asked, "What are you?"
More times than, "What's your name?"

The name Brandon
Didn't taste colored enough
It felt like cotton on black skin
Started buying triple XL shirts and
pants three times my size
Just so you know
When you weigh less than 140 pounds
Wearing a triple XL anything
Only magnifies the open spaces in your insecurities

It's hard loving yourself
When the characters you create
Become who you are
A nerd, dike, faggot
A bundle of sticks and stones
Thrown from the lips of a pastor
Can still break the brittle bones
Of a young boy trying to figure out
Why God hates him
The Bible is used way too much in tearing people down
There are people
That would say that God hates queers
But in the same breath say God is love
In Sunday school
They taught us that Jesus was a carpenter
And we are all God's workmanship
And I am sure that gay people would rather be defined by
the work of their hands
And not what they choose to do with their wood

We are all made in God's image

So God is just like my grandmother
She doesn't always respond
When we call her the first time either
God is more human than we think
Even he gave his only son up for adoption
I bet he calls himself a deadbeat dad some days

It is okay to just be
Living doesn't have to feel like you're dying
Living feels like accepting
Feels like being
Feels like love
I realized
The color of your skin isn't as important
as the hue you paint the world with
I learned to be a man
Learned to stand and shine my light
Despite their idea of blackness
Did you know
There are bees that die as soon as they give birth
I wanna live like that
I wanna live
Like my life is worth giving away

Blues for Midnight
Dasan Ahanu

Bullets are not shooting stars
Wishes and closed eyes
Have been hand in hand
Since our youth
So justice stays blind to
Imperialism's wishes that we would go away
Or stay…in our place
While society stays blindfolded by
A belief that things have actually changed

I sing a blues for midnight
Because we are still afraid of the dark
Still caught in the horror of it all
Ask Alfred Hitchcock
If he knew they shoot shadows
Sending light piecing into them
Until red signals them to stop

We lose our young at the end of rainbows
Our colored girls when it's enuf
Our young men before they can taste them
Or wash them down with a Brisk sense of satisfaction
What you want with them colors black girl
You can't have them colors black boy
You might think you as beautiful
Might think you equal
Put them colors down African child
Or we'll make the Nile run
From your momma's eyes

It is said that
Black is the absence of light
Calm collectivity
Mama said be in
By the time the streetlights came on

Because fallen angels with halogen halos
Do the devil's work
Making it easier for constellations
To be drawn across black skin

I sing a blues for midnight
Because black holes start
With collapsing stars
Even the universe knows the fate of melanin hued skin
Comet cannot cleanse dark spots
Mr. Clean is not a skinhead
We are not monsters
Bullets are not shooting stars

I sing a blues for midnight
Dancing to the melody as I march
Writing fight chants on the wind with my tongue
Listen to the airwaves
Radio Free Dixie
Nod your head to the tune
It's a party
A revolutionary party
Didn't freedom fighters teach us that
It's our civil right to resist
They knew we might not see the dawn's sun
Unless we learned how to protect the night ourselves
Past the tears falling like rain
Past the pain
Chalk outlines
And faulty media reporting

Whenever a black life is lost
I sing a blues
Call it midnight
Their families left in mourning
Their loved one will never see morning
Because somebody afraid of the dark we covered in
Afraid of ravens walking

Upon a midnight dreary
Fearing it as demon
Seeing them as birds of prey
To Kill a Mockingbird
All you need is the right excuse
And the right appearance

I got *Trouble in Mind* Nina
I asked Thelonious
What happens *Round Midnight*
He say piano lessons taught him to know the black keys
By the white ones they were surrounded by
When midnight melodies
Become funeral processionals
We remember black life
By the white one they were killed by

Ma Rainey taught us how to go on record
Stand for something, momma knows best
William Henry Lane showed us
How they really feel about black faces
I need us to learn to sing a blues for midnight
A revolutionary reverie
That inspires a radical resistance
Use our voice and presence
From the classroom to the boardroom
Senate chambers to town hall
Make *Small Talk at 125th and Lennox*
And *Across 110th Street*
Remember them *88 Seconds in Greensboro*

Sing a blues for midnight
Teach your brother and sisters
Sons and daughters
Until the melody haunts like a guilty conscious
Because bullets are not shooting stars
And the next time they invade the night sky
I might not make it home

Stix and Stones

LB

My very first breath was taken in the early hours of December 1

My very first word, according to my dad was hallelujah

The very first thing that I can ever remember learning is that God is love

My very first accident was biting a battery in half

Believe it or not growing older I would still have a taste for electricity

Something about the way it would shock your breath away

My confidant heart would let me say unbelievable things that I actually believed in

Like the very first time I said I love you to a girl

She laughed at me like a fist full of atheist

It left a bruise on my confidence the size of my first word

It swelled up my breath so bad that I didn't verbally exhale the highest praises again for two years

It taught me that my emotions are asthmatic and how much like breathing love truly is.

How being lonely and drowning can be synonymous

How fluid separation can be when words only float on air and there is no one around to sail me a reason to stop sinking in my own silence

But even when I couldn't speak God taught me to just wave my hand

Actions always spoke louder

When the very first girl told me that she loved me and meant it, it sounded like my first word

She taught me that my heartbeat is the instrumental to how true worship feels

But when the music stopped

She danced around the pieces of my heart like David

Removing every part of me until she was naked enough to find out that God is love

Even when you are not

When she told me it was over, I found myself in silence again

With no words to say I could only remember and I just waved my hand

It's funny how bye and a cry for God to save me looks exactly the same

How her name is braille to me now and every time it touches my tongue I can feel the Judas in her goodbye

The way her name sounds like 30 pieces of silver

Do you have any idea what it cost me to teach my heart to stop beating in the syllables of her name

Now I know what a goodbye feels like fighting to get out of my chest

Now I know what it feels like to fight a goodbye out of my chest

Like a back stabber

Like a fight song

Like two syllables

Like don't leave

No matter how bad being stabbed hurts you it always hurts worse pulling loves sharpness out of your life

Cupid's arrow was never designed to be removed

Especially when you love like breathing

The problem with having asthmatic emotions is that you focus too much on catching your breath

When you should be letting it go

Thank you to LaMelle, Punck Kick Slam, St. Joseph's Historic Foundation, the Hayti Heritage Center, Durham, Southern Fried, Aimee Bridges, and everyone who supports our art and us. We couldn't do this without you.

www.ingramcontent.com/pod-product-compliance
Lightning Source LLC
Chambersburg PA
CBHW071318200626
46813CB00015B/2259